A Million Miles
in my Mind

A MILLION MILES IN MY MIND

DJ McDaniel

authorHOUSE®

AuthorHouse™
1663 Liberty Drive
Bloomington, IN 47403
www.authorhouse.com
Phone: 1-800-839-8640

First published by AuthorHouse   09/01/2011

ISBN: 978-1-4634-2426-8 (sc)
ISBN: 978-1-4634-2425-1 (ebk)

Library of Congress Control Number: 2011910248

Printed in the United States of America

Any people depicted in stock imagery provided by Thinkstock are models, and such images are being used for illustrative purposes only.
Certain stock imagery © Thinkstock.

This book is printed on acid-free paper.

Preface

No two souls are the same. Life writes itself as you live it, and only you turn the page. Answers can be found only when you ask yourself first. Guidance is needed only as you allow. Asking for everything to be given to you, you're reading their book instead of writing your own. The basic outline is there for all. Right from wrong, do unto others as you wish in return. You put the words in the middle. It's the millions of pages in between for your life to be read. Rewrites along the way, this will always be, for no one is perfect. Maybe that is part of the perfection, see what changes need to be made and acting on it. This is something that we never finish as our journey continues each day. All I can leave with you is this: Live it, write it, be it.

Journey into my world where things are not what they
seem unless you want them to be.
Let our minds intertwine and our souls be free.

We create the world we live in. How those words are so true. What a bountiful journey we are about to begin when we compose our own life the way we want it to be. Just because we are not, doesn't mean we cannot be. We all have the mindset to strive for more instead of settling for less. Eyes of deception will come as you feel one way but see the other. Make sure it's your sight and not another's perception of reality. Many want you to envision their way of life and not your own. Self belief and self sacrifice share a common bond in this. Intermittently, we have to sacrifice for our own self beliefs. In turn, it will bring new light to self reliance. We cannot do it alone; although, we will try. Who can we trust that has the same beliefs as our own? Once again divided into separate societies where we choose to be. Will we ever be able to stand aside one another without feeling as if we are an unwanted element caught by each other? My world is created for the creative. Have your own thoughts for they are yours as I have mine. If you choose to share, I will listen and not discourage. What you speak I do not have to abide by, though it may change my future actions. Only a fool will not listen. It doesn't cost to lend an ear. Consequences we pay for. Far from completion is where I am. With not a worry in my mind, as I look forward for what I am about to bestow on the world ahead of me. All the answers I have not, plans I do not know, but dreams I can see.

Fear not of what we do not know for we just haven't learned yet.

Words on paper, thoughts in your mind, memories in
your heart.
Paper tears, your mind gets lost, hearts can grow apart.

Have you ever wondered how much time does one waste trying to read between the lines? What are they trying to see? The full depth? The meaning behind the meaning? For what you see, I may not. My perception might be completely different from yours. As long as you get the full value in which your curiosity desires, let it be. For your quarter, you wish to flip to decide which way to go. As I let mine roll and the destination be a mystery. Do I have a point or perhaps a question? Where I go and how I lead my life is for my own quest in which I hope to find the answer. As some will try to explain their own theory, along the way, of why I stood atop the mountain, arms open wide with a tear in my eye, or bathed naked in the salty sea as if rebirth has happened. To what array has brought this conclusion in your mind? To me it might just be a new beginning. Your eyes, my eyes, they can only see. They can not feel me nor you. You may think the acts were to become one with nature, maybe it was just to become one.

The path in which we seek is often not the one we
choose.
All things considered paths do cross.

I was standing in the middle of a dream,
With no where to run and not a soul to be seen.

All I could do is reminisce and catch a glimpse,
A glimpse of my future or what should have been perhaps.

Sights and shadows of someone into the distance were shown,
I could hear a strong voice but still not a flesh appearance to be known.

Curiosity has reached its peak,
I call firmly "Who is the one I seek?"

"It is I the one who has led your life the way you want it to be,"
I have talked to you from time to time. Are you destiny?

"Some have given me that title with which I'm named,
I'm your inner thought's actions you take on, which your life is framed".

"Some say I control them. Others think they control me,
Choices are made. Actions are taken. What ever shall be shall be."

What has my destiny left for me to do? What do I need to fulfill?
"You have all the answers. You must unlock your mind to have the power and will."

"When you think you're all alone talking to yourself,"
"I'm here to help you with life's wealth."

"Let life live itself. One's own will take care of one's own,
Hold on for the ride. Don't ever let go. Stay in your zone."

"Most of all, don't let go of your dreams and reality. They're not that far apart,
Fulfill your goals, dreams, curiosity, and most of all your heart."

As I awaken from my mystical adventure, standing in darkness, staring into a mirror, which never used to be,
All I could hear is a fading voice saying "to find your destiny, just look at the reflection and see."

How much time does one spend trying to get to that perfect place? I thought once I figured this out I would be on the right path. Just like the path, life also takes its twists and turns with an occasional dead end. It's at this very point we must decide where we went wrong. Who says we did? Some will turn back to retrace their steps where the error must have occurred. Others take it as a life experience and build a bridge to cross over whatever shall lay in their way. If it were a perfect path we travel, one would say you haven't traveled too far. It will be obstacles that will impede on our passage down life's path, and certain choices have brought us to this very predicament in which we often find ourselves. Perfection is far from me to shed light on what should be. All I can share is where I went wrong, and thankful of that I am, as it has brought on a new value of this existence. A story is something told. A journey is something we are about to embark on. An experience is a chronicle on your passage through history.

Search the world to find yourself.
Find yourself and the world will come to you.

A balcony above the shore is where I imagine myself to be,
Feeling the cool ocean breeze rushing upon my body.

As the moon pulls in the tide, my soul drifts out to sea,
Losing all consciousness and all depths of reality.

Letting life just shift among the tide,
No where to run and with no one to confide.

Soon I will be able to saunter upon the sand and swim amongst the sea,
For now I will have to watch my soul explore this existence as I feel too fragile as a body.

Alone I choose to be, to decipher my fate,
The fewer words I hear is the fewer I clean from the slate.

This disposition I've built over each year,
Must be sorted out and matched with every tear.

So I can truly know what made my soul,
Which piece fits where and which one covers the hole.

Listen to yourself while you're sitting around waiting,
Feel out the past and see your future by soul searching.

The time we spend seeking the answer from another,
Is time lost in our own true life which we should endeavor.

In this quest, one day, my soul shall return clear of pollution,
For I've seen what life is composed of and now seek redemption.

I'm only mortal. Time isn't on my side. This I cannot alter,
All I can do is live for the moment and make the best of what life has to offer.

Search throughout your life. For who you are today, you may not want to be tomorrow. Be true to thyself. The one you're misleading may be in the mirror. When will the lost be found? First we have to find what has been misplaced or if even once possessed. It's hard to lose things we never had. Even harder to find it when we do not know what we are looking for. I find myself secluded by the quest of fulfillment. Not knowing if I hold up a hand will there be someone to reach back. A little guidance is needed from time to time. If it wasn't for those in the past, we would not be here to have our instinct we have today. Is this a great endowment or curse? For what I do not know will not harm me. We've been imploded in our minds of being on top of the world for all to see. Sight goes both ways as well as sound. If you speak loud enough, they can all hear. So maybe what we desire has not been found or what we have found we do not desire. Some yearn for simplicity of life. What is theirs does not have to be yours. Make it how you want it and of it what you will. For this you've had since the foundation of life.

My perception of me,
Is often blocked by what other people see.

An outer shell is opposite from what is within,
Who decides which one matches my skin?

How often has one looked happy and felt sad,
Emotional anger wanting to burst and didn't seem mad.

Why can't I look like me and feel like you?
Things are not a hidden virtue.

You perceive a superiority one way, as I have a contrasting view,
The world is a big place with few of me and too many of you.

Your eyes are open, So use them and look around,
Somewhere a life might be found.

Try to see deep within you and even me,
We might just share the same tranquility.

When you shed your mask, I will take off mine,
Until then, the world will be walking blind.

I take the power of the pen in my hand to write my life the way I wish it to be. At times my mind feels weak and my body too fragile to make the change in this existence in which I am caught. I know now how it must feel as the elder lay in their beds just counting the days till their eyes open no more. If only they could get the words out with their fading breaths, what would we hear? Save me, let me go, or perhaps a few phrases of insight on what to expect in our aging years to come? I am able to write, as well as let the words roll freely from my tongue. I've let my mind separate from my body, instead of acting as one. I feel as if a mythological story has taken place. My body being divided amongst the four most outer places of this territory we named earth. A betrayal of myself is the only fault torn so many ways by not listening to the one who keeps me whole. Know thyself, know thy body, teach thy mind, and listen to them all. Often I imagine myself in a room without walls, as society torments my every emotion and challenges my insight. With retaliation on my mind, to let the words flow from my mouth as furious and blinding as volcanic ash. Blind their ignorance and feel my wrath, these imaginary walls keep me in. Protecting whom I'm not sure yet.

It's all I have. Just me and the words I write,
A few sweet thoughts during the day, and my precious
dreams at night.

A man of many words I can only share with you a few,
For some do not understand my point of view.

I love life and absorb all I can,
It's not much, but these words have turned this boy into a
man.

I want to grow while others stay the same,
I learn about this world while others push off the blame.

They settle for less. This I can not do,
If I took the first offer, my life would not be true.

I must refuse one to respect the other,
See my options and what life has to offer.

We must all shed our shell and come out from under,
The beautiful part about life is that it makes us wonder.

You take that and with it you build,
If you don't, you have a life in which you cannot fulfill.

Life's a journey not a trend,
It's also a book where you write the end.

Tell people what they want to hear is often what we are told. Be the person they want you to be. If you want to disregard everything you should have learned in life, go ahead. You can talk the world the way you want it to be forever. Until you act on those words, a change will not occur. Be yourself, as I choose to be me. I would walk blind before I step into a false portrayal of someone else's reality. Be as they choose you to be, an image of theirselves is what is desired. A free mind I have, the credentials I have not. A lesser caliber is what is feared. Someone from a social realm not of their own with values that stand true. Everything in which I embrace and have taken whole is now in question. Do I abandon what I have lived for over someone else's denial? Not accepted for lack of a piece of paper that tells me I am. I have to remind myself that it's just paper and just people. Both not perfect and man made. Each can change, bend, alter, and be forgotten.

Eyes of deception what do I see,
Is it my vision or your perception of reality?

Just because I am not doesn't mean I cannot be,
Unlock your two dimensional mind so you can see.

Possibilities will never cease. Opportunity is there,
Use your time wisely and be aware.

Life is there you tell me just to see,
Maybe my visions do not see your reality.

I can choose what my mind needs to learn,
In your world you have lost your turn.

What is real? Is it always by facts and touch?
Who taught you these facts and how do you know so
much?

I tell you my beliefs and you say they are not real,
Maybe you haven't learned them yet. Try to feel.

Two worlds can coexist. Some just choose to see as they are
told,
I can see both and value the one in which I hold.

Words to live by,
Do not think and do not ask why.

The place to be is where I am now,
No one really knows how.

I do not know you and you do not know me,
Let your soul dance and your dreams be free.

Over there is not here,
Live your life without fear.

Trust is just a word,
Feelings can be heard.

See with your heart and not just your eyes,
Look around once in awhile and recognize.

Life is too short for pain,
The world is yours with everything to gain.

Words are just words until you turn them into reality,
I am just your conscience not your destiny.

Silence is art. It never allows one mind to truly know another. At the right time, it can make two people reach a new beginning. As for the improper instant, it can turn lust into loath. A silent tongue speaks nothing, but yet talks of emotion. Contemplation of one's eyes can bring more truth to the conversation than the words that roll freely from the mouth. Be silent. Be still. Never fear the wrong thing to say. Let your soul speak to your voice for it will never mislead. We are art each day as we defy those who desire words of dispute. They cannot speak of what they do not know. Make them see you and then speak to you. One will talk around your mind but never want to indulge. Fear of being one step behind makes someone run instead of walk. They're missing us along the way, trying to finish a race that hasn't even begun. Be silent forever, no, but speak of you and not how someone wants you to. You are the silent voice of yesterday and the outspoken tongue of today.

You can beat me. You can cage me, but remember who I am,
A silent tongue with a memory full of freedom.

I've spoken my thoughts in the past,
My tongue became still when my visions didn't last.

Was it my time alone or this cage where you placed me?
I'm not sure right now, but in time I will be free.

When I close my eyes, this is what I see,
A place of one land, mind, and body.

You may keep me sealed in these walls for however long it may take,
I can still taste true life and will not break.

Living is a privilege, this you must learn,
Take the time to see what true life is before in these walls you burn.

I will forever be free. At least once, I had something to say,
It's time to leave the cage, unlock my tongue, and tell the world about today.

Today is the day,
I shall either stay here or walk away.

Cut myself free,
Do not let society choose who I want to be.

For I am who I am and that is something undeniable,
Do not let them take your dreams they're the only thing reliable.

Some live to dream,
Some dream to live.

Tapping your feet to the cold ground,
Living in your world where everything is just a soul to the
sound.

Where a smile is just a smile and there isn't any complicity,
Life and love where we all have the opportunity.

Stress no longer resides in this place,
You have no worries here. You can walk the race.

You can not judge one by their body for we live by our
soul,
There is no destination and not one superior role.

You never been there you say,
It's all in your cap. You just have to let your inner self drift
away.

Some go and never return for that I can see,
Others are strong enough to take this to their reality.

You're turning the ground into dust as you walk each day,
The wind will blow and make it hard to stay.

Why walk in the storm when you can ride in your dream?
You're holding the peach. All you have to do is find the
cream.

How many times have we thought about not making a mistake in our lives? A fork in the road many times we will come to. Will my life really change that much if I go the other way just once? The hardest part is finding out I was right if I had only chosen the other way. As I sit here and try to get my life on track, I hear the faint voice in the background "Daddy, I have a question"? As I search for my own solution, questions are asked of me. My uncertainties can be put on hold or just set aside. Trying to get insight on what shall come of me, I realize my future is staring back at me. My quest has changed in the sense of trying to get my life back in control. Although my life may have a little disarray I must give what wisdom I can. A child is as innocent as they come. We are the creator of how they transition. I try to instill moral values, encourage curiosity, let the mind be free. If they think they can fly, will I give them a ladder? No, but they can jump off the ground as high as they want to and I'll make them a cape. Let them known that failure is just a word, and if you speak loud enough, you will be heard. For who you are today, you do not have to be tomorrow. Opportunity knocks but you have to open the door. A child knows not of war, hate, and the impurities that are offered. They learn from us. Maybe we should learn from them. They are asking the questions of today. They will be answering the questions of tomorrow. "Daddy, I have a question." Now, what do those words mean?

A picture is worth a thousand words,
A memory worth a million more.

I have a collection of photographs,
Some with tears and some with laughs.

I keep them close at all times,
They're not much, but I know they're mine.

With these, I am never a forgotten soul,
I can look back and remember instead of being told.

I don't have them in a book, in which they are in order,
They are in my mind where there isn't any border.

They are free to roam and come about whenever they
choose,
They serve a purpose to let me know I can never lose.

For when I am down, I can look back and see,
That good does happen and evil will not forever be.

I can take a thousand pictures each day and dream a million
more each night,
My mind is the tool to let me see what is right.

To let me know that good things will come,
Your mind doesn't care what you look like or where you're
from.

It's time for me to go and dream a perfect picture of
delight,
For my visions have just begun, and I can see beauty in my
sight.

Only to awake tomorrow and take a thousand more,
I may be mistaken, but isn't that what living is for?

The impression of a heart she drew on a piece of paper,
Only to find the original in the trash later.

It was intended for me this I know,
Along with the heart was her red bow.

One she wore and would never leave behind,
Scared to look any further on what I might find.

A picture split in two,
Now I'm holding nothing, then I was holding you.

Also a tape of the song we danced to when we first met,
Although it is broken, this song is not over yet.

I'll keep that impression for when the day you return,
So we can fill it in together for I've learned.

How empty a heart without love can be,
When I close my eyes, a blank piece of paper is all I can
see.

No love, no laugh,
A picture split in two, only holding half.

So I can still look into your eyes and remember how,
It used to be, and I wish I was holding you now.

The ribbon is kept tied above the bed,
Until the day you return, and my chest is the pillow for your
head.

The song I keep singing remembering our first dance,
We will sing it together again and find romance.

We can be apart for only so long,
Our hearts will meet again and fill that piece of paper where
they belong.

Hold it close or let it go?
If you hold it too close, how can you see what you
have?

If I shall never return, remember me for who I am,
If I do return, you shall love me that much more.

For I went on a journey to seek life itself,
On my path, I discovered what I left behind was my life.

The real facts of life we live by each day,
Wanting something more out of life, but don't we all?

Our life is a song we live by,
It can be soft, slow, and sweet or run wild and cut loose.

Always at the end a ballad will begin.
To remind us what we've lost and are about to gain.

If I do not travel beyond, how will I ever know,
Whether I'm gaining a new life or leaving one behind?

If I shall find one out there waiting for me, then the sun will
shine once again.
If not, then I will return home and open my eyes, which I
had closed for so many years.

To see what is around me and what I was blinded by
before,
Walking the path of life in a circle to find its right where you
left it.

Look how much a tree changes throughout its life.
It's still a tree.

It's me. It's who I am and want to be,
We all have a choice, and I choose to be me.

I'm nothing special and about me there will never be a book,
I just live my life, and life is all I took.

I let go all the stress and worry,
Danced when I wanted to for I'm in no hurry.

I earned my way when it was needed,
Never thought twice about how I was perceived or treated.

It was done and that's the past,
I'm in a new day now, and for long it won't last.

Holding on to hate is not in my nature,
Life is too short, and death is too premature.

Time to me is merely a word,
If you spend to long looking at the clock, you won't be heard.

You will be thinking about what you should have done yesterday,
I will be bathing in the sun and living for today.

My eyes can only see what should be,
I wont judge you and don't judge me.

I've been naked in New York and bathed in the salty sea,
Danced in the rain in L.A. feeling nothing but free.

Stood atop the mountains of Denver arms open wide wishing
I could fly,
Walked across the desert of Arizona just to let the heat
waves pass by.

Running into people across the way,
Learning from some and others with nothing to say.

I spread what voice I had and what I learned,
Everyone will find their self in turn.

Me, I'm still looking. Although, I traveled further than I
thought I would,
Maybe if I turn around and try to find myself, I could.

A kiss from an angel. Could it be,
An old man just wanting to see.

That little angel one more time?
He thought it was worth every dime.

What he got was something he could feel,
A fourth generation kiss which made his life real.

Just a reminder of how sweet life can be,
I could see a sparkle in his eye that set him free.

Roaming in time to look at the past,
Childhood schemes to adult dreams making a life that would
last.

I look at him and I know. He doesn't have to say a word,
Sometimes emotions can be heard.

As a tear rolls down his cheek, every wrinkle I can see,
Each with a life filled story he has told me.

The stories I will remember. The memories I will not let go,
A kiss that set him free, and a love we all got to know.

Tell me what I want to hear,
I could listen forever,

The story of how it all began,
That's right you were there.

What happened to the child,
It was you, wasn't it?

So why did you return?
They would have never known.

There are many places to call home,
Were you scared to be alone?

You feared nothing, until they feared you,
How long before it happened?

All of it, just for that,
I wouldn't be here now, if it weren't for you then.

Was it worth all the pain?
Yes, I do have your last name.

I'm proud of what you did now, and what you did then,
when I wake tomorrow, will you tell me again.

I walk in the rain and bathe in the sun,
I will live in nature when my time is done.

One with the earth, wind, and fire,
Dreams of today will fill my future desire.

The rain will be my body as the wind will make me dance,
Thunder will be my voice, when lighting strikes my face you
can see with a glance.

I am where I belong body in the ground and soul drifting
high,
Never thought twice and didn't ask why.

Walking in the shadows of forgotten days,
You find yourself trying to get out of the maze.

Walking in darkness trying to find the right way,
Open your eyes night will turn to day.

This world is full of dreamers they say,
Who can't make it in life being that way.

I let my dreams out of my pocket so they can come true,
You may not think they're worth much, for I am I, and you
are you.

Alright take me home for I've been away too long,
Let the judging begin right from wrong.

A selfish act to satisfy my own need,
You eat from the plant as I was trying to find the seed.

Where it began and what makes it real,
You let your sight be the judge as I was trying to feel.

Trying to come back with something more,
I was exhausted always asking what for.

I want to know without explanation,
Get my own grasp and gratification.

Trying to capture a piece of time before I am caught by
fate,
Where my sanity is at question to recreate.

I come back in search of what used to exist so I could
recapture the truth,
Answers I have found what I lost was my youth.

Abandon one to gain insight on another,
Life's a broken circle without the answer.

Tuesday's past and Monday was never here,
I don't know if I'll ever see Friday this year.

I get lost further into time for each day I awake,
Life is trying to push me until I break.

I've touched the bare ground and felt the cold wind,
Seeing my hands wrinkle. Leather is becoming my skin.

Each day turns to weeks quicker than you think,
Months become years when all you did is blink.

Where has time gone what happened to my youth,
I'm scared to hear the bitter truth.

I've become what I most feared,
An old man in my twenties and my life has disappeared.

I must regain my life where the days are long,
Make one verse into a never ending song.

Let my hand touch the green fields and feel the warm air,
Where my skin is as soft as silk and living another day isn't
a dare.

Believe me, for what I say is true,
If you listen in time you will find the real you.

Take your hand, and place it upon your heart,
Feel the warmth and the beat. This is only one small part.

Close your eyes. Now, what do you see?
Is it fulfillment or is it empty?

Hush now and don't say a word,
If you listen close to yourself, there is something to be heard.

Lay your head down to rest and see where you go,
Something is wrong if you awake and do not know.

You have to listen to yourself and feel,
Bring your mind and soul together and make life real.

Live life, don't we all try?
But live it without asking why.

Touch your heart and feel your soul,
Listen to your thoughts and gain control.

Trying to find the world without knowing who you are,
You were lost before you left and traveled too far.

Find yourself and the world will come to you,
Just listen to your soul. It will know what to do.

Is it me or the clothes I wear?
I too have a heart and flesh I bare.

We are the same although we have different thoughts,
We just have different values that life has brought.

You might be taller, but we stand for the same,
To live a good life and people to respect our name.

Why do you put me down? Is it where I'm from?
I awake each day as you do and stand for freedom.

My features may vary, but my heart it does not conceal,
I am human, and it is the pain I can feel.

I don't know if I'll ever be acceptable,
What you're doing is not reasonable.

My heart can love and my eyes can see,
You once used to be me.

It's hard to start from the end,
Even harder with the message you send.

We are all one and one we shall be,
We all had to start somewhere this you can see.

Put all the anger away,
We are both here and here to stay.

'Til time tells us different and we part,
We walk this ground together both with flesh and heart.

We try to take away what little life we have left,
Savor what time we have, don't waste your last breath.

The book of me, a million miles in my mind,
What did I or shall you find?

Did you find me or were you looking for yourself?
Does it really matter if we are on the same shelf?

What I found is you must knock the dust off from time to
time,
How else can you keep your life and sanity in your mind?

What's mine is mine and yours is yours,
Although we are trying to use the same door.

Two will not fit into one, but one can be split into two,
I will go first than you can walk through.

We do not need separate places, just learn how to share
one,
Learn this then you will have your freedom.

My world is yours and yours is mine,
We own nothing but time.

Use it wisely as it does not stop or rewind,
Life is fair, but no one said it was kind.

Take every chance you get. Do not hold it in,
Opportunity is there but might not come again.

It is impossible to freeze time. The moment will not last
forever,
But you can take it with you, just dust it off from time to
time so you can remember.

The best words I ever wrote lay upon a blank piece of paper,
For once I did not write these words but chose to live them
Instead.

In order to be a great writer I must write what I live. Would you be a passenger on a plane with a pilot who's never flown? Neither should you listen to a person write about life who's never lived it. I've tried to experience what I could in my walk down society's path. Now, it's time to venture a little further into the heart of this world. See things for what they are and not what they should be. Judge not by what skill someone has but what they do with the one they posses. Reach deeper into my own self and see what I can give. They say it's not safe for someone to walk alone when they don't know where they're going. I think we all don't know where we are right now. For the few that probably do, wish they were somewhere else. One's true destination is where their soul can be found. You may walk through life all day, but your soul is running where you wish you could be. That's what I'm doing, chasing my soul. When I finally catch it, I've experienced enough for that part of my life. In this life, we will all get lost more than once and a few times, on purpose. It's just your soul, running away, telling you to chase it.